The Reluctant Deckhand

by Lorraine de Kleuver

True Story

The Reluctant Deckhand
Copyright © Lorraine de Kleuver

First Edition 2024
Published by Aly's Books

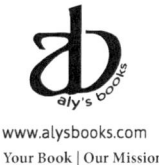

www.alysbooks.com
Your Book | Our Mission

Contact Lorraine for further copies
QR code to facebook account
or email: dekleuvers@gmail.com

All rights reserved. No part of this book may be reproduced or transmitted in any form or by any means, electronic, mechanical, photocopying or otherwise without the prior permission of the publisher.

Images are sourced from Sam Parker's and club member's private collections.

In this book, the author has recreated events, locales and conversations from memories of them. The information in this book is based on the author's knowledge, experience and opinions. All photos in the book are from the author's private collection and other parties who have supplied to the author.

ISBN: 978-0-6459030-4-1

Dedicated to

Jacobus (Co) de Kleuver

Skipper of:

Vashti – Southerly 23ft
Tineke – Northshore 28ft
No Name – Hartley 16ft
Paper Doll – Triton 24.9ft
Pax – Hartley 18ft
Purrfect – Endeavourcat 30ft

> Nothing could compare to the headspace that I was in except that of a homing pigeon.

The rip never forgives

I try to support my husband in most things; like travelling around to different places, such as flying overseas. Although the flights were boring, the places we visited were great. Even travelling within Australia in different sized caravans was challenging, but overall – great fun. Risking life and limb in a colourful balloon high above the Barossa Valley didn't faze me either. I was happy to go along with it all, until the secure feel of solid ground underfoot, fell away to the unsafe waves of the sea.

Weekends that were filled with the tastes of yummy alfresco lunches, followed with a chardonnay or a light red were replaced with nausea, vomiting and a sea sickness that had me unable to hold a glass, let alone drink anything.

Many, many times my husband tried to get me to go sailing with him, thankfully when there was no wind and lots of sunshine, then I would be happy to go and join him on his boat, but only then!

Over the years he had many boats, but there was only one boat that I liked. She was called 'Paper Doll,' and I felt safe on her. Much to my husband's annoyance I continually called yacht's, boats. He could be very much a 'Commodore' of his yacht, which at times I greatly disliked. It smacks of snobbishness, which I can't stand. So, I've always called all our yachts – boats.

I think if it wasn't for my endearment towards Paper Doll, I might not have got to experience the joys of sailing. She was a 24ft Triton, with a well-rounded body. In other words, she was small but spacious for her size. She was solid and I aways felt safe on her.

It was in Western Port Bay where I gradually got used to sailing and the 'leaning over' that boats do when pulling into the wind. Commodore was so happy when I appeared to like sailing, that he allowed me to hold the tiller and guide the boat a bit myself.

Many weekends were spent sailing and staying overnight on Paper Doll. I found that the more times I spent on the boat, the less seasick I became.

I remember, on our honeymoon we hired a boat to sail on the Whitsundays, I was seasick for three days.

The weird part was when I started to walk on land, I became a little bit unsteady, and when I went to the bathroom to put makeup on, I experienced myself swaying back and forth when trying to put my mascara on. Now, that felt really weird.

Venturing out

We sailed to various places at Western Port, but not once did Commodore suggest for us to sail around Phillip Island. Although he had sailed back and forth between the Rip and Western Port, he hadn't as yet, sailed around the Island.

I had felt safe sailing within Western Port, especially when land can be seen all the time. However, I wasn't aware that Western Port Bay was a nursery for sharks!' Ignorance is bliss at times.

So it was, on a summer's afternoon, we sailed under the Phillip Island bridge and around the Island. It was great until we re-entered into Western Port Bay. Commodore said he felt tired and asked me to take over the tiller and sail the rest of the way to Hastings.

Ordinarily I would try to help out, but for some unknown reason to me, nausea took hold of me and I quickly turned to the back of the boat and vomited my heart out. It wouldn't be the first time that I was to do that when he needed help.

Sit down and shut up!

As we got bolder and a bit more adventurous, Commodore planned for us to sail Paper Doll out from Western Port Bay, and sail her to Queenscliff. There was just one scary bit of water we had to pass through – and that was the treacherous Rip!

Commodore assured me that it will be alright – he had sailed back and forth through it many times. So, at sunrise we left Hastings marina and onwards to Port Phillip Bay.

We then motor-sailed to make sure that we'd make our way through the Rip at the right time. To not do so, would be hugely reckless with an outcome of smashing Paper Doll and drowning ourselves. Having said that about the Rip, sailing in the Bass Strait when the weather changes for the worst, is no party to be in either. As it turned out, both the Bass Strait and going through the Rip, were practically a none event. Having the times right is everything.

Even entering Queenscliff marina and mooring into our allotted spot was done with ease. All thanks to the Commodore of course. It was a real joy when we hopped off the boat and went for a walk to the nearest café, having a coffee and looking on at other boats. Great day!

The next morning, we got up early and readied ourselves for leaving Queenscliff and heading back to Western Port Bay. The trip across took about eight hours motor-sailing at about six to seven knots. So, it was with happy anticipation of returning back to Hastings marina with no problems.

Commodore undid the ropes and jumped on board to start the motor and headed out; leaving Queenscliff after having a great weekend.

As Paper Doll motored out slowly from the marina, Commodore turned the tiller towards the direction of the Rip. Feeling good and enjoying the sunrise we suddenly were thrown forward. Commodore moved to the front and took a look over the side saying, "Buggar, we've hit a sandbar."

The keel was stuck in the sand. Conscious of the time, Commodore tried every tactic he could think of to free the boat. After some time, he was able to reverse out and quickly motor towards the rip.

We had lost some time, but Commodore felt that we had enough time to get through the Rip. In earnest he motored onwards, keeping an eye out for any changes to the surface water of the Rip. As we approached closer, the motion of the water was beginning to change.

As Commodore entered the Rip with the motor on at full speed. The water was changing rapidly. Adding to that, the tide was going out, and strong winds were on the nose of Paper Doll. The waves were building up more and more. There was now, no going back. We had to keep going!

We were halfway across, but something else was at play. Commodore could feel that Paper Doll was pushing up against a force that would only get worse. Commodore now standing, and holding the tiller tightly, positioned himself so he couldn't slip or slide. Commodore was preparing Paper Doll and himself for a fight. With the motor working hard to pull us away from the dangerous waters, I could feel and see that Paper Doll was finding it hard going, as the incoming tide was pushing her towards the rocks of Port Lonsdale.

Full concentration was Commodore's priority. The two most important things were for Commodore to keep Paper Doll's bow pointing at an angle to every wave she faced. Equal to that was maintaining a firm position that kept Paper Doll from being rolled over by a side-on wave. All that, plus steering her gradually away from the rocks. It was white knuckle stuff.

Hour after hour I just watched the swell coming towards us, and then rising up with Paper Doll as she rode over them. Feelings of being scared or anxious were firmly held in place. Muscle tenseness was working overtime, keeping me tightly strung, and unmoving. That was until the waves became the height of a two storey building.

On seeing them, I swiftly moved myself and sat on the opposite side of the cockpit, where I couldn't see them anymore. Every cell in my body told me to just 'Sit Down and Shut Up!' Obediently I did just that. Incredibly I was relieved to see that Commodore and Paper Doll were slowly making progress; moving away from the rocks.

After a while I started to get my act together and decided to move across to Commodore and sit with him. As I started to cross over to him, I saw something from the corner of my eye. When I turned I couldn't believe my eyes. Dolphins were swimming within the wall of water, almost close enough to touch them. It was an amazing sight.

Eventually we were away from trouble. With Commodore's determination, and the strength of Paper Doll, they managed to pull it off! After hours and hours of punishing 'holding the line,' Commodore needed to relax, but before he did, he remembered the fishing line that he threw out earlier. As he pulled the line in he called out. "Hey, look at this!" For his efforts he was rewarded with a decent sized barracuda.

"Darling," he asked, "Can you take over the tiller for me. I need a smoke, and put this fish in the ice box." At that very same time of him asking, a wave of sea-sickness swamped over me. I couldn't hold my head up, let alone hold the tiller. With understanding, he said, "Don't worry, just let me know when you're ready." As he placed the tiller between his legs, he put his hand in his pocket, pulled out a cigarette and lit it. As I watched him draw in a long breath on his smoke, his body instantly begin to relax.

I was so proud of him, and seeing the smile on his face, I reckon he deserved every bit of feeling proud himself. No more was he just a weekend sailor of the Bay, he was now a seasoned sailor. After I recovered from my bout of sea sickness, I was able to take over the tiller from then on.

Later that afternoon he cut the fish into portions, wrapping each portion in foil with strips of thin slices of capsicum and onion, and placed it into a pressure cooker. It was a tasty dinner, with the fish just falling away from the bone.

The let down

Weekend trips to Hastings marina were becoming fewer and fewer as work commitments and work rosters were getting in the way of sailing.

Commodore found a new home for Paper Doll in Williamstown, closer to home. Alas, weekends of sailing Paper Doll was put on the back burner, and she was eventually sold. The advertisement read 'Well cared for and loved yacht for sale. That she was, and sold quickly.

Commodore was wearing many hats at the time. He got interested in computer programming as a hobby, and at work he moved away from nursing and into the area of conducting infection control audits. This had him travelling all over Victoria. Alas, he was given another portfolio, Occupational, Health and Safety. This portfolio was the one that would tip him over the edge.

OH&S turned out to be a monster, when asbestos was revealed. From the ground up, Commodore had to construct policies and god-knows what else, which in a nutshell contributed to him having a heart attack.

It really took the wind out of him, and like these things do, they make a person do a 're-think' about life, and where they see themselves in it. For the Commodore, it was spending his days sailing. At his retirement dinner he said to family, friends and colleagues, "I look forward to sailing out from the 'Heads,' and turning left; sailing to wherever."

Thus, it wasn't long before he was leafing through the Boat Sales magazines, until he found one that he really liked, and (hoped) would solve my problems of sea sickness. "Hey, have a look at this one, you won't get sick on this; it doesn't roll around as much."

"Darling I said, do not get anything that you think will suit me, just get a boat just for you." I went on further, reinforcing that "Sailing is not in my DNA." "It's not my thing." I repeated the above many times but it went in one ear and out the other.

The big sell

It was early 2013, when he found the boat of his dreams. I was happy for him, as long as he could sail it by himself. "Don't get this for me," I strongly made clear to him. "You're the one that's going to be sailing it – not me." "I'm not interested in it." "It's for you!"

Staunchly sticking to my guns of not having anything to do with going up there and sailing it back with him, was met with a resounding "NO!" "That's alright," he said, "I've got relies helping me out. One of them has even participated in a boat race from Queensland." "That's great, I'm really happy for you darling." Pleased that it was all sorted.

Assured that he now had help with sailing his boat back, he phoned the owner and placed a down payment. His intention was to fly up to Queensland to check the boat out and pay the balance then.

As it turned out, Commodore wouldn't buy it until I had a look at it with him. "For crying-out-loud" I said, "I don't know anything about boats!" A week later, after dropping off our puppy Pip at my brother and sister-in-law's place; we both were on a plane to Queensland. Hours later, we arrived at Brisbane, then hired a car; arriving at Tin Can Bay in the afternoon.

When we arrived, Kerry the owner, greeted us at the marina. He was a tall bloke, a wee bit excentric, and an all-round friendly bloke. His reason for selling was that he wanted to move back to Tasmania, to look after his father. Aside from that, he worked as a chef.

After our greeting, it was down to business, and for Commodore to be given a sail test and have time to go over the boat. While Kerry and Commodore sailed around Tin Can Bay, I was left in the cockpit. I was taken aback by its size and fit-out. It was beautiful and so airy. The boat appeared luxurious, especially against a backdrop of blue skies and all things tropical.

After the sail test, Kerry motored the boat back to its berth. Before showing Commodore around, Kerry had placed a tray of savoury pastries into the galley's oven and opened a bottle of wine on the table in the cockpit.

This guy was not new to selling boats. With aromas of savoury pastries coming out of the oven, and glasses of wine being offered; he was good salesman. He spoke about his love of sailing to quiet places to do fishing, and his reason for selling was so that he could visit his sick father in Tasmania. Knowing that the boat had sailed from America, and done a few trips in between, we could see that it was a sound boat, that had done plenty of miles.

It's always a risk when buying anything, let alone a boat. There's having the pressure to buy quickly, and we've certainly come across an array of imaginative reasons when buying previous boats.

To be fair, Commodore is no slouch when it comes to searching for faults – and of course he made sure Kerry had the boat surveyed recently. (This is usually a must). All appeared solid and safe to Commodore, so it came down to, if Commodore was happy – I was happy.

It was only whilst having coffee at the airport before going home, that we then talked about it more fully. It usually begins in talking it up – in that we convinced ourselves it was a good purchase. Then it usually ends with both of us saying that 'we done well.' Then afterwards, when we're on the plane back home, we continued to convince ourselves that we did the right thing.

Once we returned home, and collected Pip, Commodore was excited to ring his relies of the good news. I was in the bedroom and could hear his upbeat voice describing the boat over the phone to them. Then I heard a change in his voice quietly expressing deflation. I then sat on the bed listening to him repeat "Mmm," "No that's okay." "I understand" "Yep, I get it, you're busy." "No probs." "We'll catch up." I then heard the sound of his mobile phone land hard on his desk.

Hearing just what had happened, I had a mix of emotions. My heart broke for him, and at the same time, I wanted to give those arseholes, a piece of my mind. They had assured him of their help, even going on and on about their sailing experience. It was all bullshit.

Minutes later I heard the backroom sliding door open and then close quietly. I knew he was going out to have a smoke. I gave him a few minutes to be with his thoughts, before going out on the veranda to join him.

"You okay?" I asked, placing my hand on his shoulder. "What did they have to say?" I prodded. "They're not able to make time to bring the yacht down – and that they're sorry." Although he didn't convey his disappointment, I certainly expressed mine.

"Come inside, I'll make a cuppa, and we'll talk about it."

As he sat down at the table, rubbing his hand over his face, and then cupping his chin. His face had all the expressions and thoughts of 'what do I do now.' It was plain to see how deflated he was, having no answers coming forth. Unlike me, Commodore absorbs his disappointments quietly.

Despite his hurt, I became acutely aware that it might fall back on me to go with him. My mind quickly tried to find another way forward for him, and suggested, "Have a look at how much it costs to truck it down?" "It's worth having a look at least," thankful that there are trucks that do that sort of thing. That evening, Commodore was on the computer looking for trucks that that did that sort of work, and of course the costings.

We were both blown away with estimates given – enough for a deposit on a house. Trucking it down wasn't an option. It looked more and more like that I would be the bunny to go with him. As much as I enjoyed the few sails we had in Western Port Bay, it was really his hobby not mine. As much as he wanted me to share in it, it really wasn't my thing.

Unwillingly, I resigned myself to the doom that awaits being out there – in the big blue sea of endless nothingness, where even a life ring would be counterproductive to drowning quickly.

She was just a puppy

When it was time to head off to Tullamarine Airport, our playful, adorable Pip, looked up into my eyes, knowing that something was happening, and it wasn't going for a walk. You can't lie to dogs – they know when something's up – they follow you around like a fluffy ball that's stuck to your foot.

"Come on girl, jump in the car," I prompted. Pip loved to go on drives because there's always a stop at a café and a pupa chino at the end of it. This time, Commodore and I were driving her to Williamstown to get a pet carrier for the flight to Brisbane. It was important that we get the right size and specifications according to animal carriers for planes.

It was like packing for three, with all three requiring clothes, bathroom gear – generally a whole lot of stuff. There was only one item that Commodore didn't agree on me taking. I had bought one of those 'Clax' fold-up trolleys, that fold down flat. I thought it was the best thing to have when carting stuff around. What did Commodore have to say, "We don't need it." "Yes we do," I argued back.

To the ladies reading this, you just know he's going to be proven wrong – right?

"It folds down, and it's not going to get in the way of anything," I persisted. With a resigned look on his face, he realized that it didn't pay to upset the reluctant deckhand, that still wasn't happy about having to do the trip anyway.

It took us a few days for the three of us to be ready to take off to Brisbane. With a hire car we drove off to the airport. When we got there we had to take Pip to the drop off facility for pets. The poor thing didn't want to stay there, crying for us not to leave her there. Time was running against us, so I handed her to a lady that looked like she would try and calm Pip down. I felt terrible, but Commodore was pointing at his watch. We quickly got back into the waiting taxi, then on to the airport.

Once we got to Brisbane, we hired a car to pick up Pip, and then set off to Tin Can Bay. On arrival at the 'pet-pickup' facility, we were asked to follow a staff member to this big holding area. When he slid the large door open, a cacophony of deafening barks were heard from the cages of animals waiting to be picked up. After waiting, we were handed a barking Pip inside her carrier.

When I took her out of her basket she was out of control. Having been side-by-side with other dogs and being kept in the baggage area of the plane for hours, poor Pip was having (what looked like) a doggy-psychotic episode.

"Here, pass her to me," Commodore gestured, holding her harness and leash in hand. When his attempts to calm her down were failing, he suggested to take her for a walk. "I could do with a smoke anyway," he said.

As I watched them looking for a grassy area, they eventually found a spot where Pip could do a pee peacefully without the sounds of barking dogs.

After getting back into the car, Commodore said, "Let's get a coffee somewhere first." I nodded, saying, "Good idea." With Pip more settled on my lap, I was so glad that she was back with us. Poor darling, I thought. She's was probably dreaming that we were heading back home. With a deep sigh, and stroking her fur, I too thought of home – and how far away it now was.

No turning back

When we arrived at Tin Can Bay marina, Kerry (the owner) was there to greet us. He was there to hand over the keys, and give Commodore a chance to ask any further questions that he might have. Before leaving he gave us his number, and said "Don't hesitate to call me if you're not sure of anything, "Okay." "No worries, and hope your father gets better," Commodore said, waving him off.

As Kerry drove off, Commodore and I just sat down to take it all in. "Well, it's ours now," Commodore said, with a big smile on his face.

We both had another walk around the boat. Later we decided to celebrate the occasion. Kerry left a wine for us in the galley's icebox. We went to sit in the cockpit and clinked our glasses saying "Here's to our new boat!" "Do you realize that it has no name?" I said, "Well, we'll think of one on the way down."

With a spacious cabin, and a roomy galley, it looked and felt great. I was so pleased that it had a bathroom with shower and toilet. On appearances it ticked all the boxes for Commodore, and I guess for me as well; especially having shower and toilet inside.

I still have memories when on a working holiday year's before: working as a governess to a Fisherman's son. He fished around Hinchinbrook island. Back then that boat didn't have a toilet. Obviously, that boat was only designed for guys. Well, I suppose when you're on a working holiday, you've got to be ready for anything. In this case, I had to place my bum over the side, with crocs getting a full view. It was only when shining a torch over the water, that I realized how many crocs there were. But that's another story. Needless to say, I was pretty happy about the boat having a loo.

After Commodore's crash course in learning as much as he could in the few hours that Kerry gave him, he sat down and started reading his navigation book. While he was doing that, I set about getting our bags and other stuff, from the car and placing them in the boat.

That evening after having a take-away dinner, we both decided to turn in early, so that we would be energised enough to get some shopping done and return the hire car.

The next day was a beautiful Queensland day. Feeling good we took Pip for a walk, then headed off to return the car. We stopped by a café and sat outside with Pip, taking it all in, and realizing that we'll be heading home in a boat.

When we returned back to the marina, Commodore walked to the marina office to find out when was the best time to get through the rip. "The guy said "9 o'clock mate, you'll have no problems."

On return, he smiled and said, we're going tonight. The guy said 9 o'clock was the best time.

Hell's washing machine

With the help of the marina lights Commodore quietly reversed the boat out of its pen. As he guided it away slowly, he was at the same time multi-tasking his learning of the boat's instrumentation. I, at the time was standing on the foredeck, enjoying the warm breeze and looking at the other boats in the marina. That was until I noticed that our boat was quietly heading towards a row of very expensive looking boats, that were all roped up together.

I quickly shouted out to Commodore telling him, "You need to go starboard, you're heading towards those boats! He lifted his head up from the navigation screen and said, "It's okay, we're entering the channel.

Quickly I ran back to the forepeak and realised he hadn't adjusted direction. "Shit!," I thought, and ran back down to him where he sat quietly in the skipper's seat looking at the nav-screen.

I was beside myself, and snapped at him, "If you don't steer starboard right now, I will push you off that seat and be skipper myself!

He peers up, and replies, "It's alright, we're heading towards the channel." Yelling at him, I remind him that Kerry stuck close to the jetty. "Oh, and by the way, see those boats (I pointed angrily) – we're heading straight for them.

As the boat's nose was just a few metres away from crashing into them, Commodore stands up from the skipper's chair with a sigh, within seconds he quickly turns the wheel and steers the Cat instantly towards the jetty.

I was more than just annoyed, my whole body was locked and loaded to commit murder. Hearing him say, "It's alright, you don't need to go on about it," had me wishing I did.

In an effort to change the subject, I asked him what the time was. "8:30," he replied back. "We're getting close the entrance, so the rip should be nice and calm." I could sense a strong breeze and hear the sound of waves. "We're making good time," Commodore said confidently.

Away from the marina lights, the night was pitch black and the moon was covered by clouds. Motoring closer to the mouth of the Great Sandy Straits I saw another row of boats moored and roped together, positioned just inside from the entrance.

As we motored out from the bay, we entered the mouth of the rip. I couldn't see a thing. Commodore was at the wheel, looking happier that we were on our way. Pip was on my knee and I cuddled her as we sat together in the cockpit looking out into darkness. Then whack! The boat was pushed hard sideways. Then the boat was spun 360 degrees the other way. I looked out, straining my eyes to see what was happening. Pip jumped up on my chest, with her paws holding on tightly. Sounds of banging noises were coming from the sides. The boat was out of control, spinning this way and that. I tried to stand but was pushed back. "Shit, I called out!" With one arm holding tightly on to Pip, and the other holding on to the side rails, I strained my eyes for signs of anything.

"What's going on I shouted to Commodore?" He was rapidly pushing buttons on his navigation screen until he saw what was happening to us. "I don't know!" This shouldn't be happening!" he shouted back. My mind didn't have time to be frightened. Nothing was making sense to me, because I wasn't being splashed by waves. No water was coming onboard at all.

Then I heard Commodore cursing repeatedly," Shit, shit, shit!" "The rip's bloody active – shit!" Instead of us entering what we believed to be calm waters: instead, we were in a swirling whirlpool machine. Frightened, and unable to see anything around me, I grabbed hold of Pip and made my way over to Commodore.

When I saw the look on Commodore's face, I knew we were in big trouble. He was trying to figure out a way to get us out of the danger we were in. I looked at the screen with him and saw what we were facing. He instructed me to keep an eye on the flashing green and blue lights that signalled the bar entrance. "I need you to keep watch on those lights. Shout, when you don't see them."

"Sit down and hold on, I'm going try and swing us out of this mess. I braced myself, and held Pip firmly. As soon as the boat swung around outwards in the direction of the lights, he then drove the engine at full-speed, thrusting the boat out, and away from the swirling waters of the rip. I snatched another look at the screen and could see that the boat was running alongside a sand bar. It looked every bit like a pointed finger.

The swirling washing machine had stopped, but there was no way to get through, what was now a full on swirling rip. "What are we going to do? I asked. Pointing to the screen, Commodore explained that the only thing we could do, was track alongside this finger-shaped sandbar. It meant that we had to motor around to the other side of the finger. "It's going to take hours but we'll get out of it," he assured me.

Our fluffy recruit

Whilst Commodore kept an eye on our position alongside the sandbar, I tried to comfort our puppy Pip. What an horrendous way to start her puppy life with us. I kept her cuddled up within my vest, with the zip half down so she could pop her head out. When she did pop her head up, I would then say, "We're not out of it yet Pippy."

After looking out at Commodore, then at me, she would then decide to go back in the comfort of my vest and go back to sleep. Pip was barely seven months old when I got her. I say 'I' because Commodore wasn't aware of my plans to get a dog.

He was doing night shift at the time, and I wanted a dog to be around as a guard dog at home. Our street was showing signs of becoming a 'go-to' place for drugs. After watching two guys jumping over our fence, into our backyard, whilst running away from something or someone, I started feeling uncomfortable about living there. Not to mention seeing sneakers swung around electric power lines, which I found out, is a form of communication to druggies, where they can buy drugs in the area.

Emotions were multiplied when coming home from an evening shift and seeing hooded individuals coming out from laneways late at night, was enough for me to get a guard dog.

Then one day, a friend of a workmate arrived at work holding a basket of four King Charles Cavalier Puppies. They were so cute, that I wanted one immediately. However, they weren't known as a worthy guard dog.

Not to be put off, the lady handed one of the puppies for me to cuddle. I found it hard to hand her back, but I did. "I'm really sorry," I said, but I'm after a guard dog," Then my friend Eileen piped up, suggesting that little dogs are good at alerting you with their barks. That afternoon when I got her home, Commodore was not pleased.

However, when he revealed that he wanted to get a boat, I took advantage and made a deal with him. "How about you get your boat, and I can keep my dog." That week, I got her a kennel, and all the rest of the goodies that gorgeous puppies need. Last, but not least, I named her Pip. Being so full of energy and fun, It just suited her.

Alas, she and myself, never saw ourselves swirling around doing 360's in a boat, at sea, worrying about whether we were going to live or die. And every time she poked her little head out, the look from her frightened eyes, were telling me – we're going to die.

I found her such a comfort to look after, she totally took my mind off the long hours of waiting to be free from that sandbar.

It turned out that Commodore was right. As we motored into calmer waters we did get to the other side of the rip and into safe waters. It was about 08:30-09:00 in the morning when we motored past the entrance of the Great Sandy Straits, I recognised one of the boats that were moored just inside that night. It sailed through the entrance with ease.

Watching it sail out from the Great Sandy Straits trouble free, the Commodore said to himself, 'Yep,' there was a reason why they were moored there. It confirmed that the nine o'clock was actually AM hours or 09:00. The guy at the marina should have given the time in 24hr time. I suppose it could be said that the skipper should've double checked as well. Lesson learned. Shit happens sometimes! We were now safe and sailing against a beautiful backdrop of the sun rising and calm waters.

Our first stop was Mooloolaba Marina a few hours away. "Darling, Commodore asked, would you mind taking over for a while. My answer to that was vomiting over the side.

Once I recovered from that, Commodore said, "Forget it, you go and have a sleep he said, I'll wake you up in an hour. Weak and grateful, I picked up Pip who looked every bit as sick as I was. Gently I stepped down to where the cabin was, and placed Pip down on the bed. Feeling fragile I pulled a blanket over us, before giving Pip a pat. "Don't worry Pip, we're heading south now – towards home, and closed my eyes.

Whilst I was asleep, Commodore was back to getting used to Navigation equipment. Setting a course for the marina, he then worked out the time we should arrive there. Hours later we were nearing the marina. In the distance I could make out the marina wall but couldn't make out which end was the entrance, until I watched a boat entering it. Putting the binoculars down, I pointed to Commodore where the entrance was.

As much as the nav equipment indicated where sandbars were, it sometimes wasn't clear of where the entrances were. So, Commodore radioed the marina to get a berth for us.

Communication to various marinas could be via radio call signs, or hearing other boats on our radio calling marinas. Sometimes it wasn't always straight forward, info would be given by coast guard as well. It was a world that Commodore grappled with and got used to.

Once inside the marina and roping up to our berth, a wave of relief swept over me, and I'm sure it did to Commodore as well. With beaming smiles, we hugged each other and sat down in the cockpit for a brandy and dry, before Commodore walked over to the office. I took Pip for a walk and a pee and have her paws walking on grass for a change.

Once her harness was on she was off and running. We overcame the problem of Pip's toileting times. Pip learned to coincide her pee's and poo's with Commodore's smoking times, which worked out well for both. Poo's were washed off using a bucket of sea water.

This was a milestone for us, especially for Commodore. It was accelerated learning from the minute we left Tin Can Bay, that he was shouldering. To see him relaxed after a brandy and dry was great.

With a new found confidence he felt so much better in his abilities and that of the Cat. While Pip was getting stuck into her cheesy bits, Commodore announced that we have to think of a name for the boat. He was informed at the marina office that they, and all marinas down the coast, require a boat name. Registration wasn't enough.

After drinks we walked to somewhere close by to get something to eat before settling down for the evening. It took hours to figure a name for the boat, but we eventually agreed with the 'name' Purrfect.' Obviously the 'Purr' was for Cat, and 'fect' to finish the name off appropriately.

Next morning when Commodore checked us out before leaving, the guy asked, "Why did you call it Purrfect? when you've got a dog." Commodore found it easier to blame the wife and rolled his eyes.

When he told me the story, I looked down at Pip, and picked her up, saying "He's such a fibber. At least I got to name you, didn't I." Pip was such an agreeable puppy, especially when you give her a treat to get her tail wagging in the affirmative."

As it turned out Commodore had made arrangements before we left Tin

Can Bay, to finish off the rigging repairs and to fix up our main sail sheets, that were twisted and prevented the main sail being fully up. So, while Commodore waited for him, I began cleaning up and collecting any washing. After walking up to the laundry and placing washing on, I then headed to the bathrooms for a shower. After that I felt great – chipper even.

It was good to have that extra day for finding places for things, that were just thrown in when we first set off. I found the deep cold storage box worked and kept things cold really well. As I cleaned and tidied things I gradually made my way to the shower/bathroom area that had a little sink.

After cleaning the shower floor, I turned the taps on to rinse the floor. No water came out. I went to get Commodore and told him the shower's not working. So, he went down underneath the foredeck. There behind a whole lot of stuff was the tubing and related stuff for the shower. Because he was taking so long to get back to me, I sensed something was up.

I ran up to the foredeck and asked him what was happening. He said "He would have to look below the cockpit." As he tried to explain what he had to do, it was far too technical for me to understand, however for the tech heads that might be reading this, I'm going to hand you over to Commodore.

Commodore Entry:
The shower hoses had not been connected, as the boat used to have an in board motor that heated the water, but it was replaced with an outboard motor. The inboard motor and the hot water tank were removed. Thus, there was no way to heat any water for the shower until a new water tank and piping to the outboard were installed. Not something we could do until we were home.

"I hope you got all that," especially the bit where he says I can only fix it when we get home. To any female readers out there, not having a shower – when you are given the understanding that it all works! Speechless!

Once I cooled down I comforted myself that we'll be stopping at marinas with showers – all is not lost I said to myself. Pip came over to me and tried to lick my disappointment away, with her eyes saying, don't worry mummy. Her eyes conveyed that she fully understood.

The following day, after the rigging and main sail were fixed, we motored out heading towards Scarborough Harbour.

I just want to scream!

During that time at Mooloolaba, Commodore had become pretty confident in charting courses and getting our arrival times better. He estimated that we'd be there within four hours, and for a good few hours Commodore was really enjoying sailing Purrfect, and getting to use both the main sail and jib properly. He was happy and in his element. Pip and I were happy to just relax in the cockpit and just lay back in the sun, until the sun was hidden by clouds that signified that rain may be coming.

As for the precise time of arrival, we were to find out it was more a guesstimate than absolute – same as working out the weather turned out to be.

Commodore estimated a four hour trip, but he was soon to find out that a strong current was going against us, that had slowed us down from 7 knots, down to 3 knots. We had some catching up to do. Down came the sails and on with the motor was what we needed to do. Commodore was quick to get things moving.

Clouds gradually turned into real storm clouds. This wasn't good. But it wasn't necessarily bad either. We had experience in sailing in storms on Paper Doll, but we also had some protection of the bay.

Time was getting ahead of us. Late afternoon turned into evening, and the storm clouds were really pouring. Thankfully, in the large covered cockpit with clears protecting both front and sides, we were pretty much protected.

By the time we were in sight of the harbour both thunder and lightning were having a party just over us. I quickly took Pip down below and locked the cabin doors.

As we motored slowly into the harbour the nav equipment kept us away from sand bars and a small island called Gilligan's Island. Our vision was hampered by the pitch blackness of the sky. Although the nav equipment was showing us where the harbour was, we just couldn't see it.

I was getting a bit anxious, especially when Commodore was concentrating on the nav screen. The conditions became worse. I was getting frustrated with Commodore worrying about what the screen was showing and not using his own eyes. With torrential rain making it hard to see through the clears, I was yelling a few unsavoury words at Commodore. In pure frustration and anger I stepped out from the cover of the cockpit and into the storm, keeping my left hand hanging on tight to the railings.

I looked everywhere, despite thunder sounding over me. I was saturated but still tried to find some giveaway that would show me where the marina was. After a loud cracking sound of thunder happened over my head, a large burst of lightening lit up the whole of the harbour.

I shouted into the cockpit to the Commodore, "Look! Look over there!" I pointed madly. It was like night had instantly changed into day. I could see the whole harbour and the masts of boats way over the other side of the bay. Commodore stood up immediately and steered towards where we could clearly see where to go. I jumped down into the cockpit and joined Commodore.

When we finally motored into the Marina, with the whole deck lit up, we tried to find the berth that we were to go into. With choppy waters and wind making it hard for Commodore to manoeuvre the boat into the berth, I called out to him, that I'll run up front and try to get a hold of the railings. As I climbed over the railings and onto the pathway, I quickly grabbed foredeck railings. It was so close to hitting the berth structure that it didn't bear thinking about.

After Commodore tied the boat up tight and secure, we both were well and truly stuffed. As we looked around us boats of all sizes were bobbing up and down, with the strong winds howling through the riggings.

When we opened the cabin doors Pip was still in one piece shaking her tail madly when seeing us. We both gave her a round of cuddles and kisses. It must've been just as terrifying for her sliding back and forth inside.

Once we dried ourselves and fed and watered Pip, the three of us rested in the cabin. While Commodore got out the glasses and poured out a strong brandy and dry, I cut up some cheese. Now that we both could sit down comfortably, we clinked our glasses together and gave out a big sigh relief that we made it. Afterwards when we were asleep, I awoke to the sounds of padded feet entering the cabin. It was Pip, scratching to get up and onto the bed with us.

Commodore was sound asleep. I thought what the heck and picked her up. She was so happy and excited to be with us, that it took a bit settling her down to keep her in one place – which was down the end of the bed. Soon after she was snoring like a freight train. Little did I know that little minx was going to have her way sleeping with us, from that moment onwards. What can one do with such a gorgeous face looking up at you – after being terrified out of her wits.

Scarborough ended up being a great place in the sunshine and on calmer waters. The marina had lots food places within walking distance, and most of all it had a great shipwright service. This made Commodore very happy. As he was to find out the boat didn't totally get away unscathed. Again, I have Commodore with me to explain what else happened to her.

Commodore Entry
What happened to her was that the outboard pressure line that lifts the motor out of the water had a hole, and if we were sailing we couldn't lift it out of the water. A local mechanic, who fixes boats all the time, replaced the hose and repaired the old one, to use as a spare.
A sail maker also fixed the zip in the affected clear so it would not flap about – thank goodness.

Between getting Purrfect fixed up and putting up with more storms, we ended up staying at the marina for a couple of days – enough to get a good rest and get to enjoy the area a bit more. Pip had a ball with all the pats that she was getting, and meeting other dogs. That's one thing I noticed – there were a lot of boaty people with dogs.

Purrfect pain

We motor-sailed to Manley and again we weren't disappointed with the facilities at the marina. A routine started to form when stopping at marinas. It's about bathroom, laundry, fill up with fuel and water (if needed), then off to the shops and taking Pip for a walk. Purrfect also seemed to require something to be fixed. She had a flat battery, and the clears needed fixing.

After giving all my energy to clean them, I fully expected when I pulled the zip that the clears would open. I looked forward to rolling up the front clear up to let some breezes to come through. Nope, the zip wasn't going to move. Thankfully it was fixable, after spraying it with silicon along the zip line.

Once I rolled the clears up it seemed to make the cabin more spacious and breathable. Pip and I just loved sitting in the cockpit just watching everyone going about their business, which was probably fixing up their boat.

After the local electrics guy replaced the battery we were all good to go. Late that afternoon I went to zip up all the clears that I had rolled up, until I was having a tough time zipping up the main front clear to its end point. Between tugging and spraying silicone on the area, it wasn't budging. Even the Commodore tried and had no luck.

Ordinarily this wouldn't be such a big deal if the rest of the way home was going to have sunshine all the way. But as we found rain and storms kept us company on the way down. Commodore did his best to have it zipped up as far as he could; leaving an opening of about 30cm. At least inside it was fully protected, and the cockpit canvas was wide and long enough to protect us from most of the weather.

Sun, sand & kamikaze surf – skiers

From Manley we motor-sailed on the Coral Sea, and down through the quiet waters of Morton Bay. Eventually we entered the back door of the Gold Coast. As we motored past the tall holiday apartment towers that are synonymous of the Gold Coast, we also had front row seats enjoying the magnificent houses and beautifully designed gardens.

I can honestly say that we weren't ready for the Gold Coast. Having been sailing without any other boaties on both the Coral Sea, and down the quiet waters of Morton Bay; we weren't prepared for the onslaught of surf skis surrounding us. Commodore really had to slow down.

They were zooming around us, alongside us and behind. Pip didn't approve of the noisiness and barked her head off – well that was it. They all had to come and see Pip. They waved, and cried out "She's so cute." Talk about making an entry, Commodore was worried that they'd do something really stupid, resulting in us hitting them, or the other way round.

As we got closer to the marina people were standing on the pathway waving us in. As Commodore tried to get a good turn into the berth, something didn't work out, which embarrassed Commodore a bit. No-one likes to screw up in front of an audience. Thankfully some guys threw ropes to him and guided Purrfect into her pen.

As Commodore thanked them, and trying to provide an explanation, they said, "No worries mate – all good." Some boaties got talking to Commodore who were impressed with his trip coming down. As for Pip, she was in 'puppy' heaven. Kids came out from nowhere to give her a pat.

Gold Coast marina was huge. Hundreds of boats, some with coloured flags up – there were boaty people everywhere. It was late afternoon; people were lying down on the grass having drinks – just relaxing. As we walked around the marina people would smile and wave to us, and of course Pip. She was quickly becoming a celebrity.

Then, we tried to find a private spot for her to have a pee. I have to say toileting Pip did have its challenges, but the most challenge was at night. When on land I would always get a newspaper or two to place on the galley floor, but Pip being Pip, wouldn't wee on the newspaper. She would wee on the cabin floor.

It was only when getting groceries that I saw packets of those blue Chux cloths. My sewing skills kicked in creating lots of thick wee mats for her. At night I placed them on the floor in the galley. It worked, from then on the 'Chux' wee' pads were her toilet (for poos and wee). The plus side was that they washed up easy, so I could reuse them. I celebrated this 'win' as if I'd done something fantastic. It may seem like a small win, but between Pip and I, we both rested easier at night.

When it came to hanging out the laundry one had to be mindful. I found out early that hanging out one's laundry around the railings of the boat was not on. I picked up on the vibes of other boaties that it was acceptable to hang laundry at the back of the boat – definitely not at the front. I get it, it's not a good look for the marina, especially big ones that have a reputation to uphold.

I have to say though, most marinas had great amenities, so there was no need to worry, but all the same I hung Pip's wee mats on the back railings from then on.

It was such an amazing place; I was impressed with the amount of surf skis kitted out with advanced first aid gear, awaiting to answer a call. I watched a young girl get a call and run to one of the first aid Rescue Ski; racing off to help someone.

We spent a few days there, with my hard-working trolley having to go back and forth for supplies. Pip had the occasional ride in it when the walk became to long for her. Aside from our established routine of bathroom, laundry and shopping chores, another consistent became part of our daily routine, that being the job of negotiating 'sand bars.' Both the entering and exiting, in and out of most of the anchorages we stopped at.

Our next stop was a township called Ballina. They had no marina, but they did have well built places where you could tie up. Along the canal were stainless steel posts that had fold up timber platforms. It was a great idea, where you could get on/off from the boat. I thought it was pretty nifty.

However, what wasn't nifty was the sandbar. The weather was changing and it was mid to late afternoon. The waves going into Ballina's entry were pretty big in size, with a lot of force behind them. Commodore had been informed that this particular sand bar has been known to swamp boats by dumping a lot of water into the back of a boat if the engine couldn't power it through quick enough.

We watched a skipper waiting outside the entry. Commodore noticed that he was counting the waves before zooming in through the bar. After putting down his binoculars, Commodore said, "It looks like every sixth wave was a big surf wave." Looking through his binoculars again, he said "Yep, that's it." He motored Purrfect closer towards the entry. As the boat bobbed up and down – we waited.

On the rockface, people gathered along the wall, watching and waiting for us to make a move. Bloody-Hell, I thought, we need an audience – like we need a hole in the head. Pressure was on Commodore. When he was sure he was ready, he placed one hand on the steering wheel and the other hand ready to thrust the engine forward when riding that sixth wave.

I grabbed hold of Pip and held on tight to the side of the boat. As we counted, one... two... three... four... five, Commodore moved Purrfect closer... Six! Commodore pushed the engine throttle down hard on the engine, Purrfect was thrusted forward to be dead-set in the middle of the wave. Both hands working independently of each other. Purrfect was surfing this huge wave of water.

I twisted around to see behind me, the wave was higher than the cockpit – I thought we were going to get swamped, until Purrfect had pushed her nose through the entrance. Although Purrfect was out of danger, the wave wasn't finished with her yet. Before letting go of her, the wave flicked her portside corner out, making Purrfect swerve starboard, having her nose about to be pushed towards the rockwall.

Commodore quickly spun the wheel hard the other way, countering the force of the wave; wrenching Purrfect away from being smashed up against the rockwall. Once she was straightened up, Commodore could safely motor her slowly into quieter waters. "We made it!" we shouted, triggering Pip to run around our feet barking her head off.

After that, Commodore relaxed and motored Purrfect to where we were to moor up. In an effort to calm ourselves down, Commodore and I just sat and relaxed for a minute. While resting, a couple came up to us congratulating Commodore on good job getting through.

Whilst chatting with them, their dog jumped over the side and into the cockpit to play with Pip. The couple introduced themselves; the lady said she was the mayor of the township, and just wanted to welcome us. Very nice of her indeed.

After things calmed down a bit, we went inside and had our usual (sanity-saving) brandy and dry, Pip had her usual cut up cubes of cheese. All was well after a brandy, but I wondered how my body was going to hold out. Every trip thus far, had us bracing for one eventuality after another.

Meeting the locals

From Ballina we headed off to Iluka-Yamba marina. We were now leaving the Coral Sea and Queensland, and entering New South Wales and the Tasman Sea. In truth we were travelling along the coast. One of the stipulations of my being drafted into this trip was that I had to see land i.e., the coast. It was very reassuring to see land in the distance, and as a plus the trip was made more like a holiday – well, sort of a holiday.

By now Commodore was getting used to plotting a course, estimating a 'close-to' time of arrival to places, and forming a reasonable average of expected weather. Commodore used weather readings from BOM, and the predict wind app. to try and get the best estimate of weather we could expect as we headed south.

Between facing the many and varied characteristics of sandbars and the flukey weather, we were becoming 'war-ready.' Commodore didn't need to convince me of his capabilities of getting us out of a jam, and he was 'surprised,' at what I was prepared to do, let alone having resilience to get over stuff. Lucky we had brandy on board – just saying.

However, when it comes to interpretation of certain map instructions it can be difficult to identify the ways things appear. This was highlighted when we arrived to Iluka-Yamba. Commodore radioed the marina on how to get to the marina, as it wasn't so straight forward. Instructions from the marina were, turn left when you get to the first hole in the wall.

We did follow the wall but, somehow, missed the first hole and entered the second one, where we promptly hit a sandbar. While Commodore tried to free the boat, a man motored to us, offering help. After Commodore managed to free the boat from the bar, we asked, "Where is this hole in the wall to get to the marina?"

He gave us a map, and as it turned out the 'wall' was a thin line of rocks, and where there was a gap, that was the entrance. There were rocks everywhere! Thank God, a guy was fishing around there or we'd still be there. When we finally got to the marina, I fell in to what was becoming my role, jumping off the boat with rope in hand, ready to tie it to a cleat. Then next to catch another rope to fasten her stern to our berth.

A poignant moment

It turned out that Iluka-Yamba was a great marina. What they didn't have in flashy amenities, they gained in friendliness. A stand out memory for us was when we went to a local market nearby. Pip was very much still a puppy; she loved jumping about when people wanted to pat her. While we walked around looking at this and that we came to a market where I wanted to spend a little more time. Commodore just stood and waited with Pip.

Standing at one side of the stall was a little girl. She stood close to her mother, holding on to her dress, not moving and being very quiet.

While I was enjoying myself being on land, I left Commodore and Pip to themselves. When I returned I saw the mother and the little girl say their goodbye's to Pip. As I walked up to Commodore, I said "I've had a great time. I bought this," showing Commodore the jewellery I got. "What have you guys been up too?" I asked.

"It's incredible! " he said. "This lady came up and asked if her daughter could pat Pip." "I said of course, but she might jump a bit." "As the girl walked over to her, Pip just sat quietly while the girl patted her all over – even over her face. Surprisingly Pip didn't move at all."

"That's wonderful darling, I'm glad you guys had fun," but then he stopped me to say, "That's not all. Her daughter is totally blind." With the slightest of a tear showing in his eyes, he described that it was a really poignant moment, watching how careful the little girl was with Pip, and how Pip knew that she had to be very quiet and very still for her. As we walked back, Pip instantly went back to her usual playful self, jumping up on everyone and expecting a pat.

There's always a dickhead

The following day we arrived at Coffs Harbour. We mainly motor-sailed, so made good time. It was late afternoon, but the office was still open. I heard about Coffs Harbour and how beautiful it is. Because they didn't have any berths available at the marina, they gave a spot at the Fishing Co-op, close to the office. "You'll be alright there, the fishing boat that's usually there isn't expected until sometime tomorrow." During the night Co had to keep check on the ropes, to adjust them as the tide came in and out.

Early the following morning, I awoke to sounds of heavy boots going thump, thump, thump, on the roof of our cabin. "Hey!" "Get out of our spot!" a gruff voice shouted out. "This is for fishing boats!" "Get the fuck out of here now"! I sat bolt upright and got out of bed quickly. Pip was barking her head off at all the noise, and jumped down onto the floor. My heart was pumping. I pulled back the hatch so I could see what was going on.

As soon as the hatch was pushed back, this dickhead: all brawn and no brains, yelled down at me and pointing, "You shouldn't be here, now get out!" "I yelled back, the office allowed us to stay here overnight."

"I don't give a 'fuck' what they said, you get out of here now!" Commodore came up the stairs and said, "Don't worry, I'll look after this." As he made his way up to where the dickhead was standing, another guy was making his way towards the commotion. Shortly after seeing him, I then heard a car come speeding into the office driveway.

Whilst holding Pip at the window, we both watched a bloke get out quickly from the car, then run towards the dickhead still arguing with both Commodore and the other bloke who was trying to calm him down. As Pip and I listened intently, I was relieved to hear that the dickhead was beginning to calm down. The office guy then moved the discussion and dickhead to the office, and everything quietened down. Despite us paying for the spot, dickhead, not once apologised to us – thus he will remain a dickhead!

Commodore Entry
"I can tell you; it was quite a job to try and calm this fisherman down. As it turned out, the bloke that raced down to see what the commotion was about, had also rang the marina manager before leaving his boat. When the marina manager came he tried to explain to the fisherman, that he didn't expect him back until later. They've paid for the spot, so just calm

down. When he took the fisherman down to the office, he came back to us, to have a talk. He was a good guy and apologised to us. To make up for what had happened, he offered us a place that usually was not recognised as a berth. He knew that our boat; being a small catamaran, had a shallow draft, we'd be able to fit in it comfortably – at no extra charge. We stayed there for three days. It was wonderful, we were closer to everything."

Once things were settled and we now had our own unique berth, we settled down to our usual routine. The trolley was turning out to be a god send, especially when the shops were a bit of a walk away, at least we didn't have the worry about carrying it all back to the boat. We stayed there for three days. They had a bit of a park where Commodore would let Pip run around freely, but on one occasion when Commodore was bringing her back, she really bucked up about returning to the boat.

With her front paws well and truly dug in, she was determined not to go back on the boat. Commodore pulled at her to 'come on' but she wasn't having it. I was in hysterics; I was almost wetting myself. I loved her for her determination. I picked her up and gave her a big cuddle, saying "I get it! I sooo get it Pip." As I carried her back, her eyes pleaded with me, as if to say, I want to go home. She settled down of course when I gave her some cheese treats.

It was a shame that we weren't able to give the many places and towns like Coffs Harbour, more time to stay and explore outside from the marinas and harbours. Not only was I keen to get home pronto, but I didn't want to be too long away from work. Because I requested leave outside of the four weeks, and couldn't give an end date, I had to resign. The Unit Manger assured me not to worry, my job there was safe.

As usual, once we've decided when we're going to the next stop, Commodore sits at the skipper's seat, plots out our route, checks what weather forecast that we're likely to face, what size waves to expect and so forth. And as usual we're up early, to do a bit of tidy up down stairs, have breakfast and then we're off. This time we were heading to Port Macquarie.

Smiles & generosity

As forecasted it rained. As the winds were flukey Commodore decided to motor sail. Commodore didn't want to waste time as he had concerns about the engine. It wasn't running smoothly, and also our toilet was getting pretty smelly, so he needed to get that looked at. We ended up having to buy a large container of suitable chemicals to clear the loo.

Port Macquarie was something really different. It had a big public pier with shopping centres and walking paths linking up to the pier. Because Commodore was meeting a boat mechanic that afternoon at the marina, we didn't have time to look around there. As it turned out there were no berths available. As well as that, the mechanic couldn't work on the engine in the rain and postponed doing the service the following day. When we explained that we couldn't tie up anywhere, he offered for us to tie up at his workshop, where he had other boats he was servicing.

There we could use his toilet and shower facilities.

We were so grateful to him. We ended up staying for a couple of days. The guy was terrific to us and offered his work car for us to drive to the shops and have a look around Port Macquarie. We had a terrific couple of days there. Stopping off at cafes, taking Pip for walks. It was brilliant. At one café while Pip was having her pupa chino, and us indulging in cake and coffee, Pip was to have a cavies' reunion of sorts.

Coming down towards us were two older cavies, picking up their pace towards Pip, and as she turned towards them, then two other cavies raced towards her. Oh, there were tails wagging everywhere, and sniffing bums and licking each other – it was bedlam'. People inside were pointing and laughing. Passer's by had to stop and pat all of them. It was really fun, and by the time they all went their separate ways our coffees were cold. Needless to say, we got another two coffee's.

Pip had the biggest smile on her face, which indicated she wanted to see more. So, we let her take us to where she wanted to go. It seemed only fair, since all the stuff she's had to go through. It's fair to say that once the engine and toilet were sorted it was time to go. When we left, I was at the wheel taking us out but instead of going around a sandbar, I was looking at passer's by walking their dogs, until I was thrust off the skipper's seat. I had run into a sand bar. "I swear, I only looked away for a second," I explained to Commodore.

Being quite skilled at getting us out of, and away from sandbars, Commodore manoeuvred the boat out of trouble. "Now have another go," he said. "Hugely embarrassed, I snapped, alright, alright, elbowing him away from me. He sat down with Pip, saying loud enough for me to hear, "Do you reckon it's safe to sit down? Like a smart girl she said nothing, just looked away,

I can truly say that all three of us were refreshed and feeling good when we motored out from Port Macquarie. Light showers were forecasted, and on entering the Tasman sea again we were greeted with two metre swells and waves around one metre. Not bad. I suppose when one is out at sea (not the ocean), one does get used swells and waves – until they make one uncomfortable. Then that's a different story.

Our coastal motor-sailing along the coast had us being accompanied by dolphins which was always great, except for Pip. She'd be running from one side to the other side of the cockpit barking at them, until she found the Commodore's lap or my lap and decided to go to sleep.

Just keep going

What I like about Harbours is that there's no tricky sand bars to get in and out of. They're deep water, but mind you, there's a lot more traffic coming and going. Again, the skipper has to be awake, especially if you're not a local. Tuncurry-Foster (Hawk Harbour), was one such harbour. For the most part it was a stop for us to do our routine stuff. First thing we needed was fuel. Out from the marina there was a fuel station. Once again my 'trusty' trolley was able to take our fuel canisters, get them filled up, and wheel it all back to the boat.

There were a few times where we had to refuel whilst travelling. Each time we were out in open water. Commodore would get the plastic tubing and I would hold the canister whist pouring the fuel into the engine. Commodore would put the autopilot on to track us on a course that would have the boat drift away from shore.

I expect it's no different when having to refuel a car or caravan for that matter, when you're low in fuel, but have fuel tucked away in the boot or back of a van. The only difference for us is that we had a puppy that wants to stick her nose in everything. So, into the cabin she goes with doors closed. No smoking of course. Then we just work together safely and fill up the engine. I think we might've needed to refuel while at sea about three times, especially after motoring the hours that took to get us out from the Great Sandy Straits in Queensland.

Welcome protection

Newcastle Harbour – Impressive! When entering this massive port, with gigantic solid rock outcrop jutting out to greet you on both sides of the harbour is such an entrance. It was like a major highway for all sorts of boats. Incredible! Large fishing boats returning from the ocean, some were weighed down heavy, full to the max with fish coming back in.

Commodore had to be alert to everything coming in and out. I stood alongside of him to help him out. Thankfully there were huge coloured buoys bobbing about, indicating which side we could reach the harbour from.

As we motored towards the marina, there was so much action happening around us, it was a lot to take in. Eventually we arrived at the marina. Commodore had radioed in to book a berth, luckily there was one available.

Once again we got in later than we hoped. Soon after we were tied up at our berth, we got a visit from the water police to check if we were alright. Once we explained what happened, they said their goodbyes and waved us off. It was really reassuring that every time we radioed the NSW Coast Guard they were keeping an eye us as we made our way down the coast.

In fact, knowing that they checked in on us from time to time, also made us feel safe. They also got to know that we had a dog. I remember when Commodore radioed in half-way down the coast and said the usual stuff, and in answer to the question, "How many on board? Commodore replied, two adults and a dog. To which he got a reply, "Oh yea, we know about the dog." It puts a smile on your face, knowing that we weren't alone out there.

We only stayed two nights, mainly to do what needed to be done. We would've liked to stay longer but the marina was further away than what we were used to walking with Pip in tow. Even the idea of catching a taxi was out, mainly because taxi's don't take dogs.

Anyway, for me and for Pip, the quicker we got home the better we both would feel. I can't emphasise that enough. Trying to get home is one thing, but getting home in one piece is quite another – and I'm not talking about the sea, the weather and all that stuff. Being deckhand means jumping on and off piers, in storm and tempest and tying up when the boat is pulling back and forth – it's like working with a horse trying to break free against the reins.

Stupid me, I didn't think of getting proper shoes, that gave support to my ankles and arches. Brace yourself I'm about to have a winge. My knees are shattered and my arches feel like they've collapsed completely. Having declared that, I can say nothing compares to the Bitch.

Purrfect – not so perfect

You read that right – 'the Bitch'. Before even getting on a boat, I knew to expect some form of cramped conditions, but failing to be extra watchful when going down stairs, could have left me with a cracked skull.

For those readers that haven't set foot in a boat that requires you to bend your head as you enter is a given. When entering the cabin, which was wide and relatively spacious; going down stairs meant that bending your head down was imperative – if not life-saving.

The hatch is usually a timber sliding door, that when closed meets up with (in Purrfect's case) beautiful teak trimming. I met up with this beautiful teak trimming – a lot. First I'd be forgiving towards it, because it was my own stupid fault. I didn't bend my head.

There wasn't one day that my forehead didn't come head-to-head with that beautiful teak trim. Over time, my hand couldn't help whacking it back, just to make myself feel better. Then on one occasion it was busy up on deck and I had to get something for Commodore.

As I flew downstairs my forehead saw stars. The pain was unbearable. Something inside me cracked. I went to the galley, opened a cupboard door. I grabbed something that would do the job and that would make me feel better. I strode back upstairs. I turned to face the beautiful teak trim. Then with determination I smashed a stainless steel pan as hard as I could against the beautiful teak – twice. I felt so much better. Before taking the pan back, I said to it, "Not so beautiful now bitch!"

As I returned back on to the foredeck, Commodore asked, "What was all the banging about?" I bent down and pointed, "Look what that bitch did to my forehead." All he could say "Ouch! That looks sore."

I did eventually manage to keep clear of her, but found the minute that I'd relaxed and forgot to bend my head at the appropriate time, I would still want to hit her back. Call it childish, call it what you like and I'd probably agree with all of it, but I have to say, a bit of push back gets rid of all that pent-up stress.

Oh, so nice – oh so luxurious

We had now arrived into Broken Bay, heading towards Prince Alfred marina. Sounds posh? It is – and when I got to the bathrooms, I thought I was in heaven. The amenities were wonderful. When having a glorious long hot shower, I didn't want to get out. If they had had a chair in the shower I would've slept there feeling the steam relax all of my tense muscles.

They had no berths available at the time, but they allowed us to tie up against their mooring pier. And, who should be tied up on the same pier opposite us – the maxi-yacht 'Wild Oats.'

It was mid-week and pretty quiet when we arrived. Even when motoring around the Pittwater area. It was wall-to-wall boats. Houses were tucked away hidden by trees. It was quite a pretty and quiet place. After Pip's walk we booked in at the yacht club restaurant for a drink and then rest in the cockpit for a bit before going to bed.

The next day we I saw a poster at the club advertising a famous couple presenting a talk and book promotion, for that evening. The Chef organised a casual BBQ prior to the event. We enjoyed the BBQ, and afterwards went to join others and hear the talk. The couple was Lin & Larry Pardey.

Well known for their various sailing trips around the world, umpteen times, Commodore was keen to hear their stories. They not only were a lovely couple, they were a loving couple, which showed through with Lin helping Larry with the talk. Larry at the time wasn't a well man, but managed to get around and participate as much as he could. The book turned out to be the third edition Handbook regarding Storm Tactics. Commodore has read it and re-read it.

The next day we were just resting a bit. I bought Commodore a Prince Alfred marina vest. Well, you've got to buy a souvenir here and there don't we. Later that afternoon, when we went to the club for a drink, a guy got talking to Commodore, turns out he makes and sells inflatable dinghies. End result Commodore decided to buy one, believing that we might need it. Oh well, better to be prepared than not I suppose.

He kept it stored under the front deck. As it turned out, we never used it. However, all was not lost in meeting that guy. He helped us out with info on what to expect as we head south. His information on entering Refuge Cove, was invaluable in preparing us for when we get there.

The conversation was all about trusting your instruments, when your mind and what you see before you, screams at you to reverse, or turn away from the rock wall. Of course, I won't be revealing everything to you (the reader) now, sorry you have to wait.

After leaving the beautiful waters of Pittwater, we motor-sailed off towards Wollongong where we were told that they had a large pier that we could tie up on. As usual we arrived mid-afternoon.

Learning on the job

Thus far on our trip down, I had become confident in jumping up onto piers and jumping off when berthing or securing the boat. That all changed when Commodore steered us towards the Wollongong pier. For starters there was a two-story restaurant/pub with patrons all looking down onto the pier.

This was not what I wanted to see. With huge reluctance I picked up a rope and went to the forepeak getting ready for the jump. As Commodore turned the engine down, he slowly steered the boat towards the pier.

In the meantime, four guys holding their cans beer, walked out from the pub to watch. I literally wanted to die. Just before doing the jump up onto the pier, my head was screaming 'Don't fuck this up!'

Amazingly I did the jump without falling, my knees didn't give away that they felt shattered and in pain again. Then like a pro, I tied the rope onto the cleat, then walk towards Commodore, caught the back rope and pulled Purrfect towards the pier and tied her up. Pleased that I made it all look like 'Piece of cake'. That was until I jumped back into the cockpit, collapsing in a heap after keeping my nerves together, just long enough to do the job.

We didn't go to the pub, just the thought of it had my nerves shorting, besides Pip needed a walk. After the walk we stayed on the boat, had our 'nerve-healing' brandy and dry, watched the sun set, then off to bed.

The next day we headed off to Jervis Bay, where Commodore's nav-equipment showed that Cabbage Tree Point; tucked well inside of the bay, was a good place to anchor off. It was pouring rain and when turning in we were facing southerlies, which was a nuisance as the front clears didn't zip up fully.

I was using our laptop to assist Commodore. The whole time, whilst keeping the laptop dry so I could tell the commodore how he was tracking. All the while having the rain and the loose clear flapping in my face. Eventually we got to Cabbage Tree Point.

Commodore let off the anchor to moor overnight. Close by, a guy was fishing from his boat. After waving and saying hello to each other, he called out, "Are you a local here?" "No, we replied." "Okay, just letting you know that your mooring's not safe, you'll drift off overnight. He then showed Commodore where to anchor instead. Commodore was very appreciative of his help.

One of the things I admired about Commodore, if he wasn't sure about something, he wouldn't hesitate to ask, or allow someone to help him. People, in general especially locals are only too pleased to help out, especially when it looks like you might need it.

Even though he had experience at mooring off at places – they were places that he knew pretty well. On this journey, he was literally learning stuff on the go, but he didn't have local knowledge. I think overall, by the end of the journey, we'll both be experts.

Moving On – Ever Closer

After our overnight stay at Jervis Bay, we headed off to another public pier at Ulladulla. We were gathering a fair bit of knowledge and confidence when facing different sandbars and tying up against varying public piers. When we arrived at Ulladulla we were told to tie up alongside to a fishing boat. We were initially a bit apprehensive, remembering our experience back at Coffs Harbour, but it turned out to be a comfortable overnight stay.

Having a run of overnight stays picked up the pace in getting us closer to home. So, we decided keep doing overnighters at both Ulladulla and Bateman's Bay, in an effort to shorten the days to get to Victoria.

Keeping us company during the hours of motor sailing, were groups of dolphins. I think our boat gave them something to play with for a change. They were ducking and diving alongside us and in front of us. Pip had got used to them and no longer barked at them. All the same though she kept close eye on them, and when they got too close she then would bark at them.

As we got closer to Bermagui, the coast guard warned us of the entrance. The coast guard strongly emphasised how tricky this bar was. We had to motor up close to the rock wall, then when nearing the corner of the rock wall, Commodore had to do a very sharp turn, which avoided the bar and got us in calm water again.

It was a fantastic day, calm and sunny. We were instructed to tie up to the fishing trawler named 'Devocean.' There was no way we could miss it, it was massive. There was no crew on board, as we found out, it was there for repairs.

It was no mean feat having to go to and from shops and for walks. We had climb up and over the sides to get to the deck which was big. And do the same on the return trip. Taking the trolley was not an option, it was too awkward.

Pip had to be carried, which she thought was fun, because she had a big smile on her face, each time Commodore had to pick her up. For a change of pace, we decided to stay a couple of days and rest up. Bermagui was a pretty place with some nice shops. Of course I bought things, especially maritime looking things. Anything that gave the boat a 'homey' look. Commodore didn't say anything, he too wanted to get home just as quick as me, before I started thinking of turning the boat into a house.

Bermagui turned out to be great fun. We stayed there a couple of nights, and we were lucky that they had a late shopping festival. All the shops were open. They closed the roads off. There were all sorts of market stalls and activities for kids, and people walking their dogs. One such dog was too much for Pip. It was a massive Swiss Mountain dog.

When he first went over to her, his fur coat covered her completely. She was having no more of that and decided to play dead. She refused to move with the dog there, so Commodore had to pick her up. When we got back to the boat, and sat down for our 'usual.' Pip had her nose to the brandy; almost saying to us, 'after what she went through, she should have a brandy as well. Try as she may, she had to settle for her cheese cubes.

Before Commodore went to bed, he sat with his nav-equipment plotting a course that would take us into Victorian waters! I picked up Pip and did a little dance, singing, "We're almost home," repeatedly.

Chance meeting

Before going to bed, Commodore plotted a course to somewhere special – a National Park. The next two days we were going to have fair weather. We set off to Gabo Island.

We met a Park Ranger who said we could tie up there. We asked about our dog Pip, and he said that we were to keep her on a leash at all times and that 'we' were not to go anywhere near any rookeries. He spoke about what they do there in regards to protecting penguins, shore birds and vegetation. We kept our walk with Pip fairly close to where the boat was, and when we wanted to walk a bit further we placed Pip inside the cabin, with the doors closed.

Whilst walking around we met a guy that was also staying on the Island. He waved to us, and came over. He saw our boat and started chatting about sailing. He was an experienced sailor, and offered some advice. He told us that when we've done the leg across from Gabo Island to Lakes Entrance, it's worth refuelling at Port Welshpool before you do the next leg to Refuge Cove.

When returning back to Pip and the boat, we felt rejuvenated from the walk. It's such a rugged and windy place. With the ocean on one side with crashing waves, then on the other side is the mainland blowing warm air across the water. It was summer and the mainland was enjoying warm and sunny day.

The longest day

We set off from Gabo Island Jetty at 05:00 hrs, ready for the long day ahead. The forecast was SW Winds at 10-15 knots. Commodore plotted a course to have us arrive at Lakes Entrance at 18:00 hrs, when the tide would be okay to enter the bar.

An hour after leaving Gabo Island, the winds changed dramatically becoming much stronger, and the waves increasing in size to about two metres. Gradually things got worse having the winds face on the nose. Purrfect was a strong boat and pushed through, having sea spray and waves constantly battering us. Hour after hour we gradually made slow progress towards Lakes Entrance. By 16:00 hrs Commodore said, "We're not going to make it to the bar on time, and that we wouldn't arrive there before 21:00 hrs.

While I took over the wheel, Commodore radioed in to Paynesville Coast Guard to explain our predicament. The guy said if you find yourself in trouble call triple 000, but before Commodore was about to call triple 000, he received a call back from the Paynesville Coast Guard, providing the direct number to the Lakes Entrance Coast Guard.

After calling Lakes, the guy that answered was really helpful and understanding. He told us to keep going, until we were five minutes out from the entrance. Once Commodore was relieved, he immediately had a wave of sea-sickness, no doubt with the build-up of tiredness and worry. When we got the next call from Lakes I took over the radio while Commodore was spending time bent over the side of the boat.

When I explained to the coast guard how we were, he said that he had things in hand and that a crew member would board us and take us in. I breathed a sigh of relief and passed on the news to Commodore. I stood by the wheel and turned on the deck lights; to show most of the boat brightly. Then I turned the engine down to idle. Poor Commodore was truly done in. Pip moaned when Commodore lurched his head over the side yet again. She stayed with him, looking up at him every so often.

As I waited and listened by the radio, I could hear several radio calls of other boaties requiring help. Lakes Coastguard were pretty busy that night. There were many other boats apart from us, requiring help.

After getting a blanket for Commodore, Pip stayed snuggled up to him. As for me, I was looking up at totally dark skies with no stars to light things up a bit. I tried to see where the other stranded boats were, but no other lights could I see. Incredibly I wasn't sea sick at all, but remained tense, constantly looking for any sign of light from other boats.

It was 22:00 hrs before I received a radio call from the coast guard. He was checking in to see how we were going. I said that the skipper is still sick, and that I couldn't see any light from where we were. Soon enough I saw a strong light coming towards us. What happened next was nothing short of amazing.

Within seconds they sided their boat alongside us. Then a big bloke quickly came aboard and straight away took over the wheel, put the throttle down and sped off. When we got close to the entrance, it looked as if he was driving us nose first into a rock wall. I was about to yell out, when all of a sudden he made a sharp turn, then forward out into the calm waters.

Then he motored the boat to a pier and tied her up securely. He was not only incredible, the whole time he was assuring us that we'll be okay. Before leaving, he bent over and said to Commodore, "You okay skipper?" as he gave him a tap on shoulder. "You did good skip, you'll be alright now," and jumped off, running off to join the other coast guards.

Commodore went to bed, while I turned deck lights off, then closed up the cabin doors. Then placed Pip's wee mats on the galley floor. Soon after, I heard Pip race up the steps, scratch at the bed for me to pick her up and place her on the bed. All I could hear was the lapping of the water against the sides of the boat. Seconds later I was asleep. It was 23:00 hrs when we got in – it was the longest day in my life.

As we woke up to a sunny and warm day, we got up feeling pretty rough. Commodore felt a lot better, saying that he couldn't get over that he got seasick. "It was quite a night," he said.

After breakfast he decided to go and have a shower and a shave. I decided to clean up a bit and collect stuff for the wash. It was only when Commodore returned that I found out the usual set up of laundry being next to bathrooms that I had got used to, was a nice walk away, about 15-20 minutes down the main street, and there was no laundry. However, when we got a berth, I found a laundry called 'Spin City,' was situated close by to our berth. As for the shower, I decided to just have a wash at the sink, until we get to the next place.

Lakes Entrance; for anyone that doesn't know it, it is home to a huge fishing fleet. Aside from that, it has a lot of great places to eat and a couple of big supermarkets. It's one of Victoria's holiday places and gateway to the lakes district.

We stayed there for a few days, which gave us time to catch up with our God daughter, who was living at Lakes Entrance. After having a meal at the pub across the road, we finished the rest of the afternoon mucking around with Naomi's dogs and Pip at a nearby park. Later, as we walked back to the boat, it wasn't lost on me that we were only three hours (by car), away from home.

When we settled down at the cockpit for our evening brandy and dry, we just relaxed watching people walk along the esplanade with their pets. Pip was happy just to give the occasional bark. When it was time to turn in, I told Commodore, I'm not walking to the shower, I'll just have an APC wash. Once the kettle boiled I took it to the sink and soaped up the face washer. For the uninitiated, an APC wash stands for armpits and crutch. I placed my nightie and towel on to a hook before washing myself.

As I rose my arm up to soap it up I saw in my peripheral vision something moving. I turned to look closer and saw a face looking at me, still not sure, I wiped my eyes and looked again. I yelled out. In seconds armpits and crutch fell instantly to the floor. Pip rushed in when she heard me. Then Commodore came in. "What's wrong," he asked, while I was trying to reach towel. Pointing upwards to the window, I said, there's a pervert at the window. "I don't think so," he said. "There is!" I snapped.

"Do you want me to have a look," in a tone that he was too tired to bother. "Yes, I do," getting more snappier by the minute. So reluctantly he went back out. "Hello," I heard him say to someone." I could hear him chatting away to whoever. When he returned he said, "It's just a fisherman, fishing on the pontoon." "Well did you tell him off?" "He got another towel and tried to hang it across the window, which fell down. "Just hold it up until I finished, I snapped again.

That night I had a solution. As soon as the shops opened, I went to a stationery shop, bought thick paper, then got it laminated. Went back to the boat, cut the laminate into shape and placed it onto the window. I stood back and said, "That'll do it!"

Feeling quite proud, I showed Commodore, "Well, what do you reckon?" I shouldn't have asked, his reply was "How am I going to open the window?" I replied. "Men! "I should've pushed you overboard last night!" as I shoved him aside.

Eyes in the dark

The next morning, we decided to have another rest day. After a coffee and taking Pip for a walk, Commodore came by a shop called Voyager Electrics, which had AIS.

Commodore knew of it, but hadn't investigated it further. What was obvious to me, that Commodore was really interested to know more about it. Because it was all tech stuff, I left him there and took Pip back to the boat.

This is where I will hand you over to Commodore, as he can explain it better than me. I'll catch up again when Commodore is finished;

Commadore Entry
AIS = Automatic Identification System, This allows us to exchange information on Navigation, Heading and Location with other boats and the coastguard.
As we were in a very busy sea lane it made it safer to be able to let other ships know where we are, and equally important the big ships can see us and can warn us to get out of their way.

"Hope you got all that," because it turned out to be really useful, and was instrumental in Commodore convincing me to do a night sail when leaving Lakes Entrance.

Under the stars

Against my better judgement, I went along with what he wanted to do. It was one of those balmy nights where the sunset was so beautiful and Lakes was wonderfully calm.

Better still, when going out through the entrance was a non-event. Even the sea was as calm as I've ever seen it. We had enough fuel to get to Port Welshpool, so we both felt good when leaving.

For the night sail we set up a box for overnight, with a thermos of hot water, milk, tea, coffee, and biscuits to have in the cockpit. We also had the laptop that showed our co-ordinates, and what was around us as Purrfect motor-sailed along.

Unfortunately, our satnav (satellite navigation), wasn't holding a course setting very well. Commodore became aware of it when he was trying to work out why our time estimates were always out. Since then, we both were at the skipper's chair steering the wheel most of the time.

I was the first bunny to take first watch. I didn't mind as I had the sunset shift. The colours were amazing and with the quiet sounds of the engine taking us out along the coast, southward – closer to home. Pip stayed with me for a time, then decided to go downstairs and keep Commodore company. When my two hours were up, Commodore's alarm went off. After he made his coffee, I kissed him good night, then went to bed myself.

We kept to our shifts, and I couldn't believe how lucky we were just quietly motoring along. The AIS kept me entertained for a time, seeing that we were passing big gas platforms and such. The main worry, and why Commodore got AIS, was so we could see where the big cargo ships were. We were told that those big ships cut the 'corner'(Wilsons Prom), pretty close. For us, by the time we could see a big ship, you have to be pretty quick to move away from their path – as their engines are fast and powerful.

When sunrise rose, it was still magic. It was an unbelievable night trip, and around breakfast time we arrived at the entrance of Port Welshpool. It was low tide and we could see the many shallow areas. Fishermen in their dinghy's were motoring back and forth to fishing spots. I was surprised on how long it took motoring all the way into Port Welshpool. It took hours. By lunch time we arrived and I got out and climbed the ladder to tie Purrfect to the pier.

Pip was keen to go for a walk, so once Commodore checked that the boat was secure, we walked along the pier pushing our trolley with fuel canisters towards what we believed was the township.

You're kidding me

We saw a fuel bowser and started to fill one of the canisters. Nothing happened. A little shop was open and Commodore walked in to let the person inside know that when they were ready, we wanted to fill up our canisters. "Sorry Mate, that bowser has been closed for some time now." "Where's the nearest place I can get fuel," asked Commodore. "In the township, up the road," the guy said. "Is there a taxi," I can call?" "I'm sorry mate, there's no taxi service around here, or in the town.

The township was small, and twenty K's-plus away. To say that I was pissed-off would be an understatement. We walked Pip back to the boat. Commodore checked the fuel gauge. We are really low, and we don't have near enough to get to the Refuge Cove, and we can't get fuel there either. There was only one choice, we had to leave Pip in the cabin, and we'll take the trolley and walk. It was really hot when we took off down the road towards the town.

My anger about the whole thing had me marching along the road hoping that a car would come along and be kind enough to drive into the town. We had been walking for over 30 minutes when we passed a house that had their sprinklers on. We heard voices in the garden. Commodore suggested that we ask them if they would take us into town, especially having fuel canisters to fill up.

I personally didn't fancy his chances, but he called out from their boundary fence. A lady came to the fence, and listened to him. Then she called out to her husband to get his work van, and take the Commodore to the petrol station in town. Before she finished, she called out to her husband saying, "And, don't take any money from him, you hear?"

Commodore was very thankful and got in the guy's van. I walked back to the boat and Pip, where I tried to keep cool inside the cabin. When Commodore returned with the trolley with canisters all full with fuel, I was so happy. Commodore offered money to the driver, and he said, "You heard my wife, but it will help pay for the petrol." Commodore was only too happy to pay – they got us out of a real pickle.

After lunch, Commodore went to get the laptop and read more about the AIS software. When he picked it up he saw that the cable had been chewed. "Pip!" he called out. Pip knew she was in trouble and ran up the steps and out into the cockpit to where I was sitting." "What's wrong?" I asked. He held up the cable. "God, I can't get replacement cable until we get to home."

As I mentioned early in the story, about Commodore keeping his emotions internally, however, I did hear him grumbling as he went downstairs. I looked at Pip and said, "You're lucky you didn't chew anything of mine missy, or you'd be in the water by now," nodding to her. With that, she walked to the opposite side of the cockpit, and snorted as she slumped herself down on the seat. You know the way dogs do, place both paws under their chin, with eyes of innocence – 'yep,' you know what I mean.

Commodore not sure how he could fix it, phoned our friend Marshall, who lived in Drouin, to ask him what could be done. Being a couple of hours away he suggested that he'd drive to Lakes tomorrow with a cable and see what he could do. Commodore felt more hopeful, as we were yet to get around the corner (Wilson's Prom), and he wanted to be sure that we'd get warning when a big ship cuts the corner close.

That evening we decided to have dinner at the local pub. After giving Pip her cheese and a bit of chicken, we left her in the cabin. While walking down the pier we noticed a big fishing trawler berthed at the harbour. When entering the pub, I recognised the guy waiting at the counter and asked Commodore, "Isn't that the guy from Voyager Electrics at Lakes?" Commodore said, "Hi Mick, what're you doing here?" He replied, "I'm doing a job on that trawler over there," pointing over to it.

When he went over to a table, Commodore suggested for him to join us. During the evening Commodore told him about Pip, and what she had done. He laughed and said that he'll look at what cables he's got in his van after dinner. The long and the short of it was, Mick ended up repairing our cable, and gave us a shorter one, saying, "You can have this, just in case Pip wants seconds.

Later, Commodore rang Marshall about the luck we had and that we were okay. That night, as we sat back having a late brandy and dry, we talked about how close Christmas was, and that he was hopeful that we'd make it to Flinders in time for having Christmas dinner with our friends in Rosebud. "You know I said, I think we've had all our Christmases at once." We've been so lucky." "I'll say 'Cheers,' to that as we clinked our glasses.

The next morning, feeling so much better knowing that we had plenty of fuel to get us to a place that had such a reputation of being both beautiful and scary. It was with some trepidation the we headed out from Port Welshpool and onto Refuge Cove.

The secret door

It was on a sunny, and calm day when we motor-sailed out from Port Welshpool. We had a bit of a breeze and calm waters. We were feeling more positive now that we had fuel. The trip to Refuge Cove was a relative short trip. Commodore put out a bit of sail to pick up a the breezes. He placed the satnav on a course towards where we were going, with the intention of occasionally keeping check if we needed to reset it.

While Commodore got back to reading Lin and Larry's book on Storm Tactics, I just laid back in the cockpit, resting on comfy cushions, when Pip plonked herself in between us, watching out for those pesky dolphins.

It was early midday when Commodore pulled in the sail and became more active. "We're nearing the entrance he said as he hopped onto the skipper's seat. As he slowed the engine down, Purrfect entered what appeared to be an alcove surrounded by a rockwall. The sun was shining revealing the whole alcove, but there was no entrance to be seen.

Commodore placed the engine on low. Purrfect was now just idling, small waves just lapping at her sides. Commodore was just standing, holding onto the wheel. Aside from the lapping sounds on the boat, everything was so quiet. On all appearances we were largely surrounded by a huge rock wall. Commodore looked at his instruments then at the wall. I couldn't see any opening, or even a hint of an opening in the wall.

"Well, everyone I've talked to has said trust your instruments, the cove awaits on the other side of the wall, but you have to get up close to the wall to see the opening."

"Well... my brain is telling me not too, but here goes," he said, as he increased the engine carefully. The nose of Purrfect headed straight towards the rockwall. I don't know what Commodore was feeling, but my whole body tensed up. As we were almost at the wall I called out, "Stop!" But then, all of a sudden there it was — a large gap opened up revealing a beautiful blue water cove. As we motored further inside, we saw three other boats anchored quietly on the water. Such a huge wave of relief swept over me that I had to sit down.

We both looked at each other laughing. With a brief hug given to each other. Commodore motored to a place that gave us space from the other boat and let the anchor out until it stopped, then pulling up any loose chain.

There we were, surrounded by the beauty that was part of Wilson's Prom. As we waved and called out "hello," to the other boaty people we collapsed inside the cockpit. "I'm glad that the sea wasn't rough, because I would've fainted," I said to Commodore. "Don't worry, I was holding my breath the whole time," he replied, as he headed down to the galley reaching in for a bottle of wine. Within minutes he was pouring wine into glasses saying, "I don't care what time it is – Cheers!" he said as we clinked our glasses to being alive.

Later, a lady came over in her dinghy to let us know that that there is no wireless cover here, except on the hill she pointed, that was on the other side of the cove. She further went on to say that she or her husband will be taking their dinghy across to the shore around 5pm. "We're happy to take one of you across with us, if you want phone anyone," she said.

Commodore thanked her, and said that he would like to make a call, when they're ready. "How lovely of her, to offer that," I said. As it turned out the lady was taking two others over to the shore, where they would walk up the hill, and try together to get a call through. Pip and I thought it quite funny watching Commodore and the others holding their mobile phones up high trying to get a call through.

However, it wasn't only mobiles that would be affected, it also affected our nav equipment. Commodore wasn't getting a clear reading of tidal flow and wind readings. The Cove was so well protected it didn't give us any idea what the winds were like outside of the Cove. That meant, for us at least, that we would have to go out from the protected cove to get an idea of what the sea was like.

The next morning the weather seemed okay, until we went further away from the cove. The waves weren't friendly and neither were the winds, the boat was being lifted up and then slammed down repeatedly. I was at the wheel at the time, and said, I wanted to persist, until we got around the corner, but Commodore was having none of that, and took over the wheel and turned the boat around swiftly. As he turned on the downside of a big wave, we were so close to being flipped over. Like the time when Commodore surfed in over a bar on the 6th wave at Ballina. He held his nerve and surfed Purrfect over the bar and out of trouble. He did the same then.

It would be true to say that I had a moment of madness and frustration with a totally unrealistic fear of the outcome. We were so close to home – if only we could get around that bloody corner.

Once back inside the protection of the Cove, Commodore tried to cheer me up. I was at that stage that I wanted to punch a wall in. I was fed up with the boat, fed up with the endless troubles, fed up in being confined to a limited space, and totally angry that there wasn't a wall to punch in. Then Pip bravely came up to me, and placed a paw on my knee. She looked up at me with those eyes of hers, sending me a message, 'I get it mummy – I totally get it.

For tea that night, I pulled out the hand-made sausages that two guys that we befriended at Lakes gave us: we fried them with a can of diced tomatoes, sliced onions and cut up long beans. I needed some comfort food, and of course a glass of red, well maybe two. Later I went to bed dreaming of home and worrying about the garden being dry.

The next morning, I had my fingers crossed that the weather outside the Cove would be friendlier than the day before. Commodore took the wheel, while I sat with Pip in the cockpit. We were two days off from Christmas day, and we said to our friends in Rosebud that we'll try hard to get there on time. We knew not to make any promises on anything, as we proved all the way down, we were always arriving late.

As per usual, the winds were against us, but on the whole the weather was reasonable. We had turned the corner. Commodore decided to take a selfie of us rounding as we motor-sailed passed the lighthouse and rounding the corner. It was a horrible photo. Both of us hadn't showered since leaving Lakes Entrance. Commodore was scruffy and I didn't have 'my day face' on. (Only women of my age will understand that). We should've taken a photo of Pip going around the corner instead.

Omen's warning

We were now on the Bass Strait. "We're in home territory now," Commodore said, with a smile from ear-to-ear. He was happy, we were on the homeward straight. The plan was to be at Flinders at a reasonable time for our friends to pick us up.

Commodore decided to go further out when rounding the corner: that is Wilson's Prom. He knew of the short cut, but he'd heard of stories of sailors getting caught there, so he didn't want to take any chances.

It was a real grey day, and cool enough for us to have our jackets on. Weather forecast was for light rain, so that's okay. In the distance there was a large rock that appeared to be round and smooth. As we motored closer, it looked like a rounded rock with nothing significant about it. That was until we motored past it. As we moved along the other side of it, it gradually took the shape and appearance of a skull. With the hollowed out eyes, nose and cheeks it looked pretty convincing – a place for pirates and smugglers of old. Surrounded by grey and gloomy sky, and even darker waters, it was enough to give you the shivers and turn the motor up and zoom off.

"Commodore," I said, "That rock looks every bit like a skull." "Yea, I know, it's called Skull Rock. "Well, thanks for 'not' giving me the heads-up about it. At least Pip was giving me some comfort while she snored on my lap. The more I looked at it, I wondered to myself, I hope this is not a bloody Omen. If my Nana was on board, she'd be definitely thinking it was an omen. She was Scottish, and was a very superstitious woman.

When my brother and I stayed with her for some time, I remember her saying things such as; "Don't put new shoes on a table—it's bad luck. She had numerous sayings that all had bad or good luck attached to them. Here's another; do not place a kitchen knife on top of another kitchen knife—it's bad luck, and the weirdest one of all, was watching her throwing salt over her shoulder, straight after she accidently spilt salt on the floor.

Anyway, I tried to raise my thoughts away from all that stuff and stare out across the water which looked twice as bleak and eerie as Skull Rock. Thankfully, after a while the grey sky gave way to a sunny day, and the Bass Strait was on its best behaviour; nice and calm. Commodore would've been happier if there was more of a breeze so he could hoist the sails up.

When passing the cliffs of Cape Paterson, memories of Wonthaggi came to mind of my dad and brother surf fishing along the beach, and of the many times walking back forth over the sand dunes, to get something out from the car, which was an arduous walk. One thing I can say to you, is that I never would've thought that one day, I would be sailing on the other side of the cliffs of Cape Paterson.

Finally, hours later we were making good time, but as always when we got closer to our destination, sunset would show itself, then nightfall would close in. When entering Western Port Bay, I rang our friends in Rosebud, that we were going to be late, and that it would be best if they picked us up the following day.

The wind had started to pick up when we entered the bay, making the waves short, but choppy. We decided to stay overnight at Flinders, because it was getting late, and we were both tired. It had been another long day and both of us were keen to tie up at the Flinders' pier.

Commodore looked at his nav equipment and noticed that we couldn't just motor through the middle as there was an aqua farm of some sort, that had boundaries where we would have to go around it. No problem. That was until Commodore's attention fell on the enormous warning lights on Flinders rockface entrance.

For some reason, perhaps tiredness was at play, but Commodore became fixated on it, so much so, that he believed that we should be steering towards it.

It was the largest coastal warning sign that I had ever seen. To me, it was like a pattern of large-sized asterisk's, that were so well lit, making them visually screaming at boaties to stay away from it. Commodore had a bit of a think, then steered the wheel towards the warning sign, saying "We'll turn this way."

"I don't think so, I said, if anything we should be keeping away from it." I was a bit perplexed why he would see it any other way, other than a really big warning sign.

When he repeated again for us to go towards it, I started to get concerned. The trouble was that there were so many lights flashing in front of us that it became confusing. We were at the entrance just idling the boat until Commodore assured himself of what's what.

Across the entrance I could see lights that flash on and off, as per the timing set for them. Then there were the lights showing the outer boundary of the aqua farm. Then there are the mooring lights that boats have on. To the uninitiated it can be a bit full on. Commodore had not been through Flinders at night, and it might've thrown him a bit.

Then after a minute or two, he steered towards the warning sign again, and said "We're going this way, sounding every bit that he had made his mind up. "No!" I said firmly, "Just let me get my bearings for a minute." He stopped and kept the boat idling. I could see he was getting frustrated with me. I scanned what was in front of me, until I noticed the tiniest form of lights that were quite a distance away. What was different about them is they were static. A small line of lights that were positioned to look like the letter 'L' laying horizontal. "I can see it!" I shouted, as the wind blew around us.

"There's the pier," I pointed out to him. He stared our across the water. "No, it's not!," he persisted, it's this way, he pointed towards the warning sign again. My voice and temper were climbing. "That is not the way, the pier is this way. I'm certain of it," I strongly emphasised.

"That's not where the pier is, he repeated sternly, adding we have to go this way, pointing again towards the rockface." I knew he had totally lost the plot by then. What followed next, was an extreme example of when Fright, Flight and Fear, take over when a person believes that they are in mortal danger of losing their life.

My decision was made. Out from the darkness and in the howling wind, shouted a loud and threatening voice. "If You Don't Fucking Go In That Direction," (my hand pointing angrily towards the pier), "I Will Fucking Take Over the Wheel Myself!"

Shocked, at having me speak to him like that, he said, "Alright, you don't have to swear at me." I just turned away shaking my head and clenching my fist – hard. "Commodore, (probably feeling like he's been verbally tasered), smartly steered the boat towards the tiny lights in the far distance that I was pointing too.

What seemed like ages, the pier slowly revealed itself. Elated that I was right, I so wanted to parade around the deck saying, "I was right, I was right,' but I didn't. Instead, I turned and looked at a man that wasn't well. I could see he was truly knackered, and probably became disoriented for that time of confusion. What was becoming apparent to me during this trip that Commodore had lost weight. I could see it in his face and upper body, that he was becoming gaunt looking.

As much as we worked as a team along the journey, Commodore was the skipper; responsible for everything. If anything went wrong with the boat, he had to fix it, and with all the ports we stopped at, he had the worries of getting in and out of them. Other matters of plotting our journey, keeping check on weather forecasts, and all the other worries that the sea throws up, had built up inside him.

After that episode, the build-up of those stresses he was internalizing were showing themselves – and the 'sea-sickness' at Lakes, was every bit related to his internalising his stress. Worst of all, not admitting to it, and surrender to taking a rest. 'Men!' They're their own worst enemy. As for me, I had my girlfriend Kerry, at the end of my mobile phone. Twice, I called her and her husband John, to come and pick me up. "I've had enough!" "I want to get off this nightmare." Like a homing pigeon – I just wanted to 'be' home.

Christmas Cheer

After a good sleep, the two of us felt much better and were more civil towards each other. Before getting breakfast ready, I took hold of Pip to give her cuddle and see how she was. Out of three of us that night, poor Pip got the worst of it. When things were getting a bit rough while motoring to the pier, I placed Pip in the cabin and closed the door. Hours later, when opening the cabin doors, all I saw was a frightened Pip with poo all over her fur, and the rest of the cabin had loose shit from pillar to post. Yep, it was a mess.

"Come here girl," I said, "It's all right, It's not your fault," I said to her softly, as I reached for a towel to wrap her in. I went straight to the ice box and reached for the cheese. By that time Commodore was stepping into the cockpit. Before he got any further, I handed Pip to him, and some slices of cheese. "We've had an accident," I said as I handed Pip to him to look after her, while I clean up the mess. As I closed the doors, I could see her starting to settle a bit while Commodore was looking after her.

I have to say, that the Chux Super Wipes and a bit of detergent, worked a treat in cleaning the cabin. I handed a bucket of warm soapy water for Commodore to clean up Pip's fur, and by midnight we finally made our way to bed.

The next morning it was Christmas Day. We woke up to a lovely sunny day. Commodore called our friends, apologising for not calling the night before. "All good, said John, I've got to pick up some things for Kerry, so I'll pick you guys up on the way.

He didn't take long, so we had time to have a shower at their place, (Thank God!). Lovely hot showers are the best thing, especially when you feel half dead. Once dressed, I felt human again. Kerry, had everything else pretty much organized. Their son Tom, was helping out where he could. When it was a bit quiet, Kerry took out some drinks and nibbles out onto the balcony where the sun was coming in, and where everyone sat down to relax.

I could feel every taught muscle unwind and relax. I felt good – and relieved that we had made it. We only had Queenscliff and Williamstown left before making it home. Being surrounded by Christmas decorations and the aromas of Christmas dinner wafting out to the balcony, lifted my spirits. Commodore looked ten times better, and Pip was just sitting in the middle of all of us.

Between her and their dog Mack; those two had a brilliant time getting spoilt. Then Kerry's Mum and friend entered, and it was all kisses and hugs all round, leading up to the main course of Christmas lunch. Our day, couldn't have been any better. It was wonderful.

We stayed overnight with them and slept in a 'real' bed that didn't roll from side to side, or have the sounds of rigging hitting the mast all the time. I was in heaven, and fell fast asleep before Commodore and Pip, started snoring.

The last Leg

The next morning John dropped us off at Flinders, and we headed inside the boat We intended to motor-sail to Queenscliff that day. That was until something changed our minds. A big stormfront was heading right for the mainland. The Queenscliff idea was rubbed out, replaced with a quick dash towards Hastings to shelter there.

Next morning, the weather had toned down – comfortable enough to motor-sail towards Port Phillip Bay. Commodore did a quick check of the tides from the BOM website, which reported slack tide at the 'Heads,' at 13:00 hrs.

At 06:00 hrs, we set off from Hastings and headed out from Western Port Bay, where we were met with winds on the nose again, and another choppy ride to the Heads. Despite that we arrived at the 'Rip,' at the right time for once. Just to be sure, Commodore decided to call the Coast Guard to check on conditions of the Rip, and was told that "Well, at the moment the rip is running out at 16 knots. He then said, "You can go through if you like, but slack tide is actually at 16:00 hrs. Commodore wasn't impressed.

I wasn't impressed and neither was Pip. She got to know what our faces looked like when we get pissed-off at something. For the next three hours we just had to sit and wait until then. So, when Commodore slumped down in the cockpit, then I'd do the same and Pip would follow, except she was cuter with her two front paws supporting her face, but she would snort her disapproval.

Commodore wanting to do something, motored us out to a safe area, where we would just bob up and down, until then. Every so often he would re-adjust things accordingly.

Commodore and I would swap and take a nap, and it must've been during those times that Pip decided to have a wander. (Possibly to have a pee).

After some time, I saw Pip just casually jump into the cockpit, from being at the front of the boat. She must've been going up and down to the motion of the waves all that time.

When I saw her, I almost had a heart attack, and instantly grabbed her. In all that time, I believed her to be safe in the cabin, but I didn't have the door closed. That little minx must've snuck up and wandered off to the front. I kept an eye on her after that, all the while thinking that we could've lost her.

Eventually, we could go through the Rip, and when Commodore fired up the engine to motor through, we were met with a wall of murderous skippers willing to run us over if we didn't get out their way.

It was the Melbourne to Devonport Yacht Race. We didn't know where to steer; right or left, or just close our eyes and hope for the best. To think hundreds of boats jostling for front position for hours, sails at the ready, waiting for the entrance to be safe to get through. And what do they meet when they burst through – a bloody cat! It was either get out the way or we'll run you over!

Happiness is a dog that can smell home

Due to being held up outside the 'Heads' for the three hours, we knew we'd get in late to Williamstown. "Let's find a berth at Queenscliff," Commodore suggested. I was only too happy, and luckily for us, they did have a berth available.

Queenscliff was our happy 'go-to' place when on days off. It had everything for us. Situated on the shores of Port Phillip Bay, it had a top-notch marina, with great amenities, great cafes, restaurants, parks, and a maritime museum, plus a community of stingrays that call the marina home. Queenscliff has the whole box and dice, and we loved doing day trips there.

When we berthed up and secured Purrfect, Pip couldn't wait to get out. She knew where she was, and if it was market day, she would have shot off to the Pet treats' stall, where she'd strain at her leash to pull us there.

With her tail wagging she had the biggest smile. She knew the places to go, and more importantly – where we would go too. Pupa chino for her, lattes for us and a piece of bacon from our egg and bacon toasties that we'd give her. We might not have been quite home, but for Pip this was home for now.

After the café, Pip immediately took us to her favourite places before going back to the cockpit of Purrfect. As the three of us sat, relaxed and watching people walk by, I looked over at Commodore drinking his wine. He was relaxed, and happy that we made it. I was happy for him, and it's fair to say that I was happy that we actually got through it all, and still in one piece.

"Congratulations darling, I said cheerily, You've done it!" I held my glass up across the table to him, and said "Cheers!" Our two glasses clinked. Conversation was no longer about the next marina, the next pier, the next bloody sandbar. It was being relieved that we made it, and having fun with Pip.

Commodore Last Word:
Sometime later I joined the local coast guard and this was one of our first callouts.

It was late afternoon when I received a call about a boat that was slowly sinking with four people on board, in Port Phillip Bay. I remember joining the team and racing off to where the incident was reported. When we found them, their boat was full of water and all four people hanging onto the sides of the boat, in the icy cold waters. We took them onboard and back to shore. It was a timely reminder how dangerous the bay can be, and of course the benefit of having a volunteer coastguard.

Message from Author

When writing this story – I wasn't sure how I was going to approach it; mainly because it wasn't the best of times for me. Especially when I was brought to situations of extreme stress. I can laugh and joke about those times now, but I never want to go through any of it again.

Other than being a story of a reluctant deckhand (myself), I've found it's also a story that has twists and turns that can apply to anybody. For instance, being thrust out of our comfort zones, having to negotiate on so many things that one may totally disagree with – and to be prepared to step in when you have too. The main tools that have to be mastered is to Respect each other, be prepared to work as a Team; honouring that a Team practises 'give' and 'take.'

Acknowledgements

It goes without saying that we didn't do this trip by ourselves without any help. As the story attests; there were many people that helped us when we were in trouble. Whether it was local advice, driving us to get fuel, helping us out with electrics, repairs to the boat and so much more – we owe all of them a 'Big Thank you.'

And last, but not least, we give a big 'Shout Out,' to the Coast Guards of Queensland, New South Wales and Victoria – we couldn't have made it back home without you all.

A Poem

To never be content without
the things that you really care about,
to strive for them
to never doubt...
this is to have a dream!

To feel that you are truly free
to shape a new reality,
where everything can come to be
this is to have a dream!

'A Sailor's Dream'

by Co de Kleuver

Postscript:
You may remember me mentioning my concerns about getting back to work, in the least amount of time. Well, unbeknown to me, the Premier of Victoria during that time, was on a mission to sell off 800 public health beds. I was working in mental health, where I was part of a fabulous team pushing through barriers and exploring different ways in providing great quality care for our clients. On my return, that facility was sold off. Losing a job is one thing, but it was a real shame that so much more was lost.

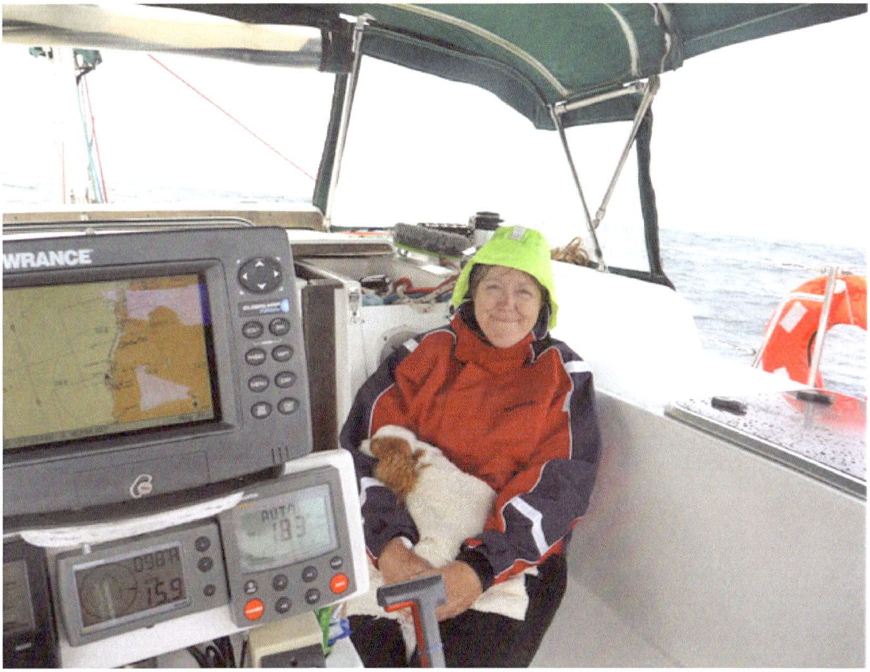
WRANCE
AUTO

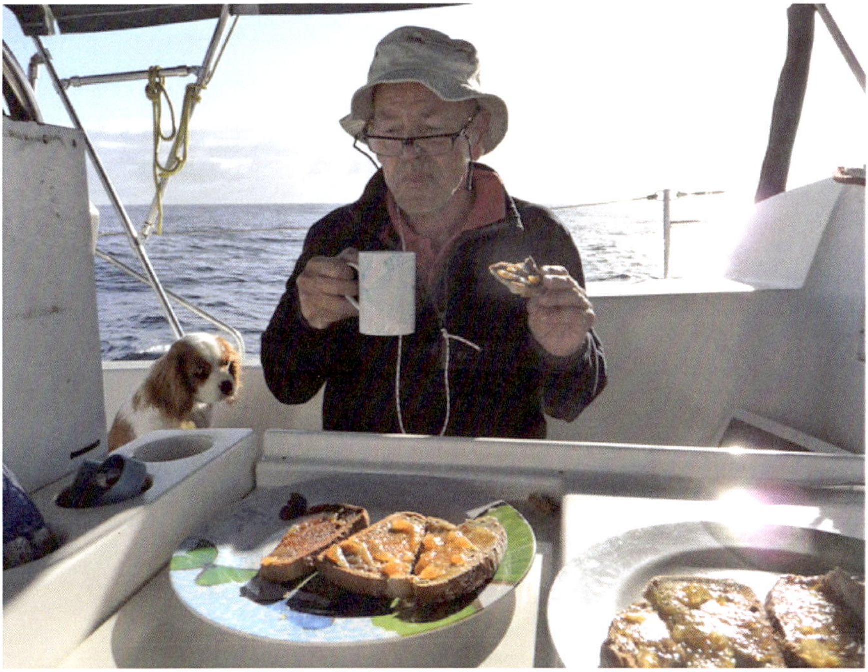

www.ingramcontent.com/pod-product-compliance
Lightning Source LLC
Chambersburg PA
CBRC091957300426
44109CB00007BA/160